Learn to 1
5
STRING
BASS
By Mike Hiland

MW01201524

Online Audio

www.melbay.com/94721BCDEB

AUDIO CONTENTS

2 3 4 5 6 7 8 9 0

Contents

Foreword

Welcome to the world of 5-string bass!! You are either reading this book due to your recent purchase of a 5-string bass (congratulations!) or because you decided it was about time you learned a little bit more about the 5-string you are already playing. Either way, I'm glad you're reading!!

The 5-string bass is relatively new to the music world, but it has made a very big splash in a very short period of time. Everywhere you look, you see 5-strings: country, jazz, rock, pop, heavy metal, virtually any kind of music you encounter or listen to. Almost every music store that sells basses has at least one 5-string hanging on the wall. What's that tell ya?

So, now the question is, "Why do so many players play 5-string?" The answer is simple: The expanded tonal range. The 5-string bass goes lower than the conventional 4-string.

It should be noted that some 5-strings have the 5th string above the G string tuned to either B or C. Since that is a much more rare form of using the 5-string, that tuning is not addressed in this book. The concepts still apply. There are just no explicit examples of using the 5th string above the G string.

"How do I use this expanded range?" is the next question you should be asking. I'll show ya!! This book includes an explanation of how to read the additional notes that come with the 5th string, finger exercises to get you used to the string spacing, a complete study of scales and chord tones, tricks to use on the 5-string, slap exercises, and numerous musical examples in a bunch of different styles! Everything but teaching you how to play bass. I assume you already know how to do that!

This book is designed to help "open your eyes" to the additional tonal opportunities that the 5-string provides. It is my hope that the combination of the information in this book and the knowledge you already have will help you realize the full potential of the 5-string bass. And if we're lucky, we may even have some fun along the way!! So, let's get to it!

A quick "thank you" to Mr. William Bay for all of the great opportunities he has given me. Also, thanks to George and Gloria and everyone at Kaye's Music Scene. And a special thanks to my brother Dan for all his support and encouragement — we'll get there bro'.... And now, *on with the show!!!!!*

Mike.....

Reading

Reading the notes on the 5-string is really "no big deal." You need to learn only three more notes: B, C, and D. That will cover the open 5th string up to the 4th fret on the 5th string. Since the 5th string is tuned to B, it is a 4th below the E string. Therefore, the 5th fret on the B string will be the note E. As the A on the 5th fret of the E string is the same as the open A string, the E on the 5th fret of the B string is the same as the open E string.

From a reading standpoint, every note above the 5th fret on the B string is the same as the notes on the E string. That is, the 6th fret on the B string is the same F as the 1st fret on the E string. The 7th fret on the B string is the same F♯ as the 2nd fret of the E string. It's that simple!!

Here are the notes on the first 5 frets of the B string:

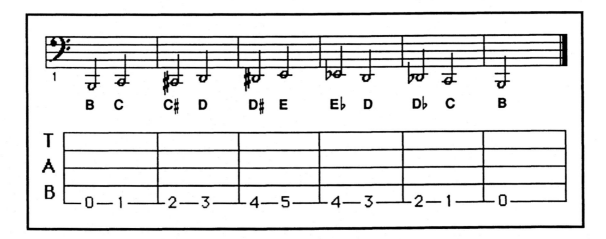

Now we have a few little "pieces" (ha-ha) to help you learn these new notes. Some of them are played completely on the B string, while others just "dip" down onto the B string. All in all, these should help you get a good start on reading the notes on the B string. If you really want to master them, practice reading piano music. Many left-hand parts on the piano are written in this range. For now, let's do these:

Reading Ex 1

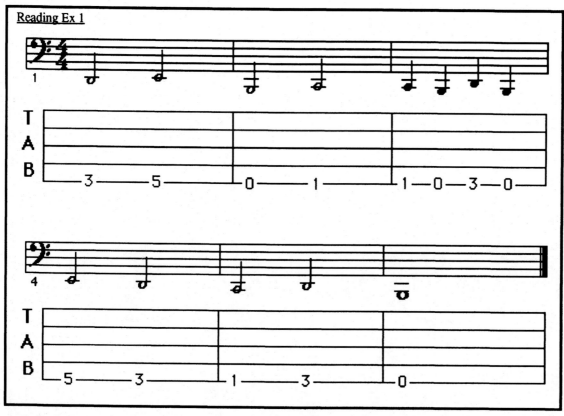

Reading Ex 2

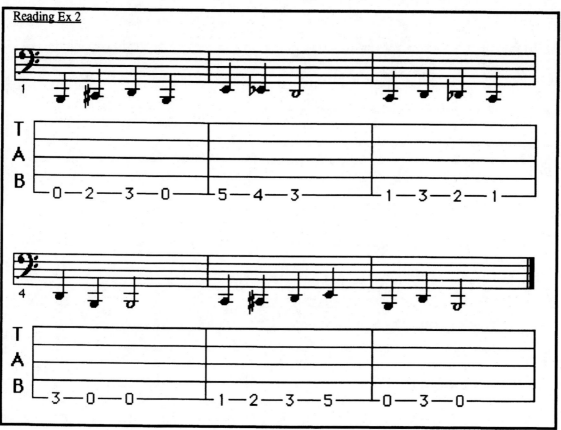

Reading Ex 3

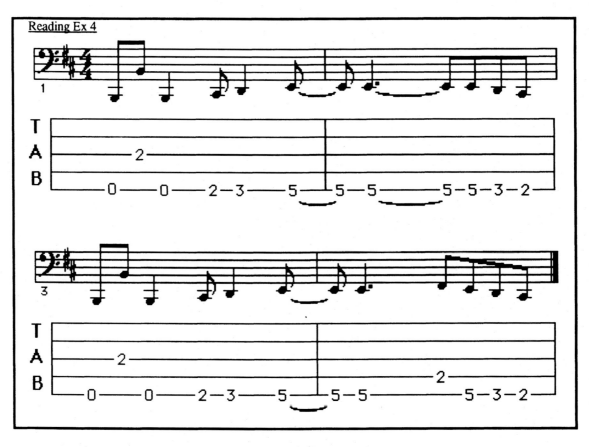

Reading Ex 4

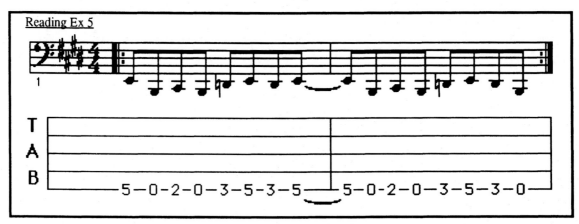

Reading Ex 5

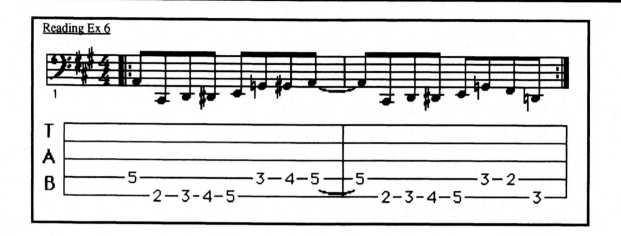

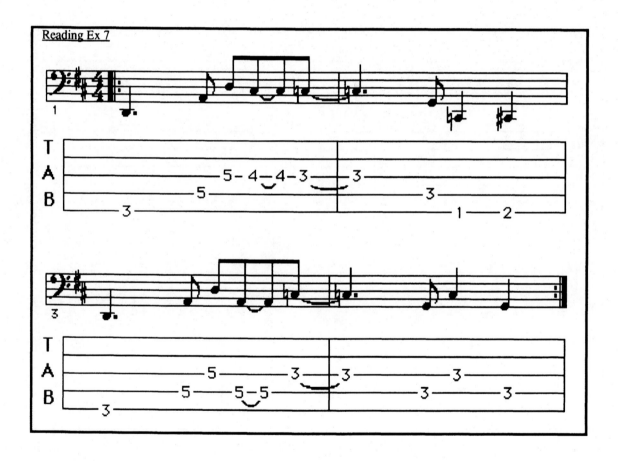

Exercises

Most 5-string basses have string spacing that is closer together than normal 4-string spacing. This can result in a fairly "clumsy" playing technique if you're not careful. I have laid out some exercises that stress playing across the strings as opposed to playing chromatically (on the same string). This will help you get used to the string spacing of your 5-string.

When you play these exercises, be sure that the technique that you are normally comfortable with is not altered, or at least not altered so that you become uncomfortable playing on the 5th string. You may need to learn a little more about using your left thumb as a "pivot" in order to reach the 5th string. And you should try to keep your fingers close to the fretboard and keep both hands relaxed at all times.

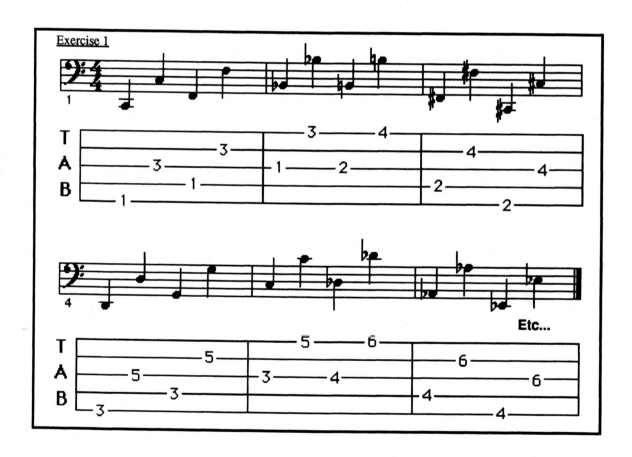

Exercise 2

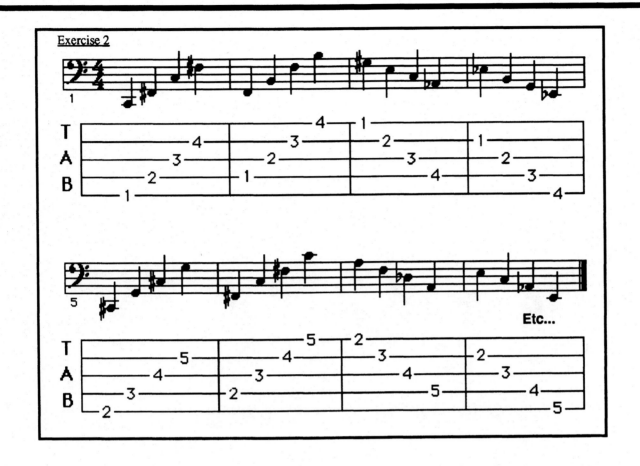

Etc...

Exercise 3

Exercise 4

Exercise 5

Etc...

Musical Examples

Here are a few examples of how you might use the 5th string. Once again, these examples are not based solely on the 5th string. Instead they are intended to demonstrate a few ways to *incorporate* the 5th string into your everyday bass playing. As I mentioned in the foreword, the 5-string bass is not a "new" instrument. It is a "new" version of a 4-string bass. Therefore, we need to learn how to incorporate those new features into our playing.

More bass lines can be found in later chapters. Hopefully, these will just whet your appetite a little......

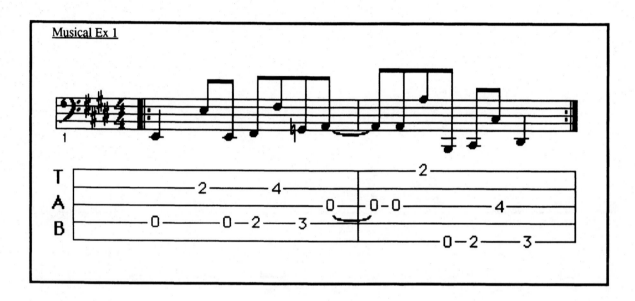

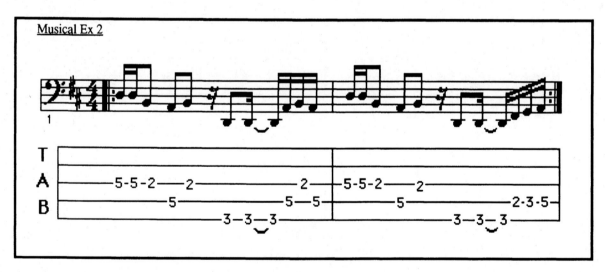

Musical Ex 3

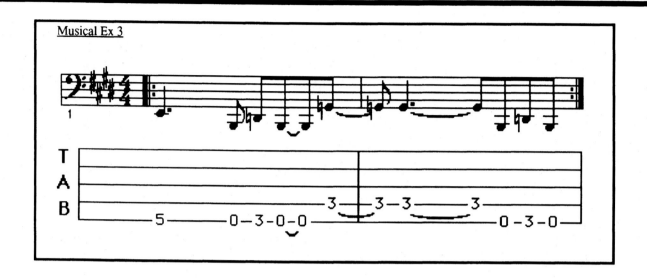

Musical Ex 4

Scales

Scales. Now we're gettin' down to the nitty-gritty of the advantages of 5-string bass! The expanded range that is allowed by the addition of the 5th string is most evident when you study scale patterns. As you will see, in many 4-fret and 5-fret positions, you have an additional octave!

In this chapter, we'll look at four different scales and how they lie over the fretboard. The scales covered will be the **major, major pentatonic, minor,** and **minor pentatonic** scales. These are the most commonly used scales in popular music. Besides, once you are familiar with the major and minor scales, you can use that knowledge to locate and play any other scale you desire.

MAJOR SCALES

We'll use the **C major scale** to demonstrate a major scale which is **rooted** on the 5th string. After that, we'll talk about scales that are not rooted on the 5th string. It is important to understand how to use the 5th string in both types of scale situations.

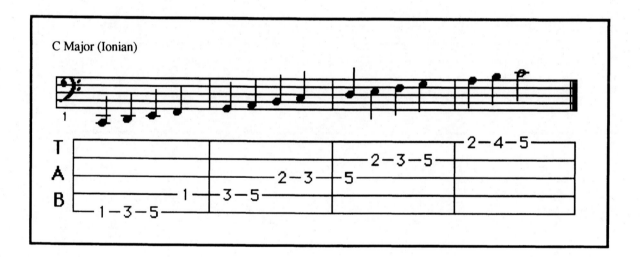

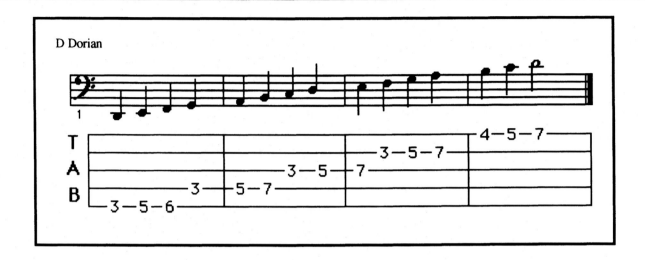

D Dorian

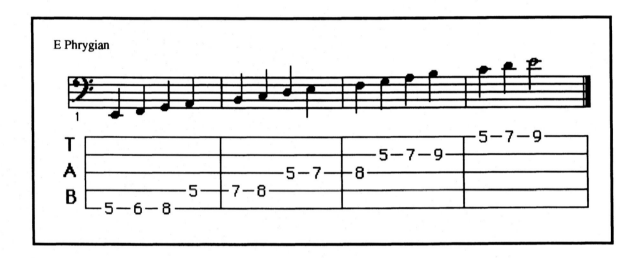

E Phrygian

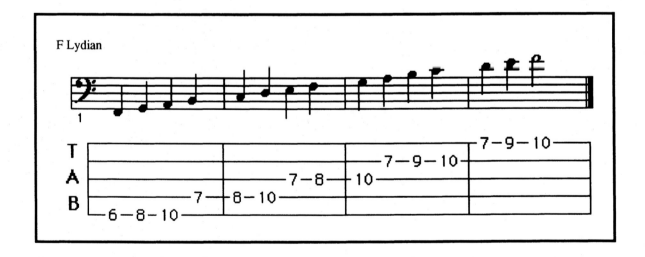

F Lydian

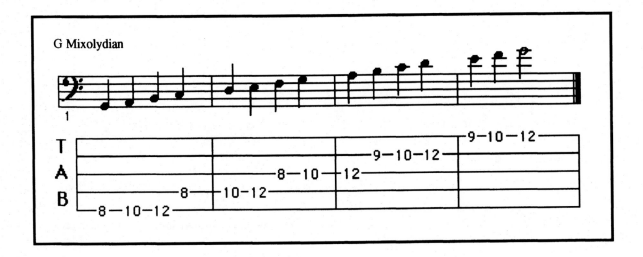

G Mixolydian

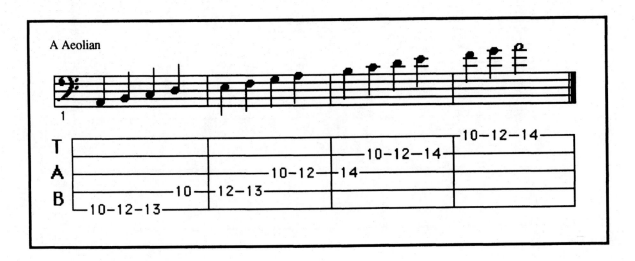

A Aeolian

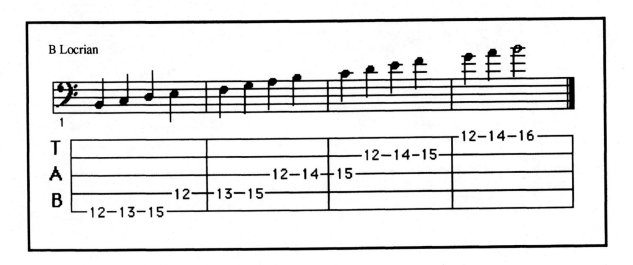

B Locrian

When playing a major scale that is not rooted on the 5th string (relative to the neck position in which you are playing), it is important to be aware of the scale tones that lie on the 5th string. Let's look at the **A major scale**, rooted at the 5th fret on the E string.

Here are two variations on the A major scale, the only difference being the range of the position. Do yourself a favor, and expand this scale all the way up the neck (at least one full octave) to help you fully understand the relationship between the 5th string and the rest of the scale.

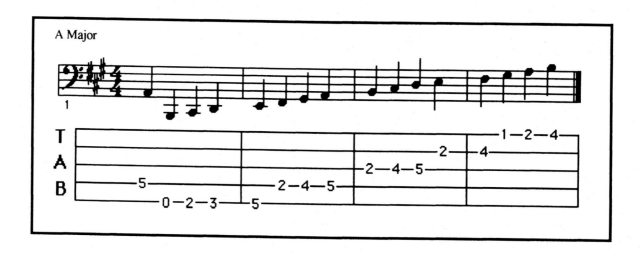

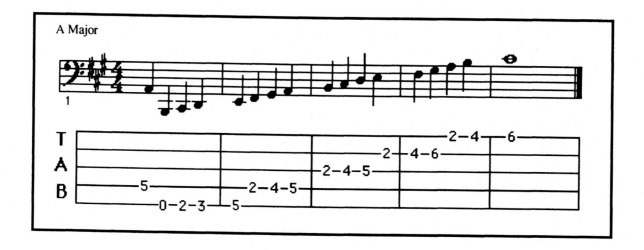

In order to help *burn into your brain* all of the scale patterns in this book, I recommend playing each and every one of them as shown in the following two exercises. The **motif** of each exercise should be fairly obvious, so you should be able to apply each scale pattern to each exercise.

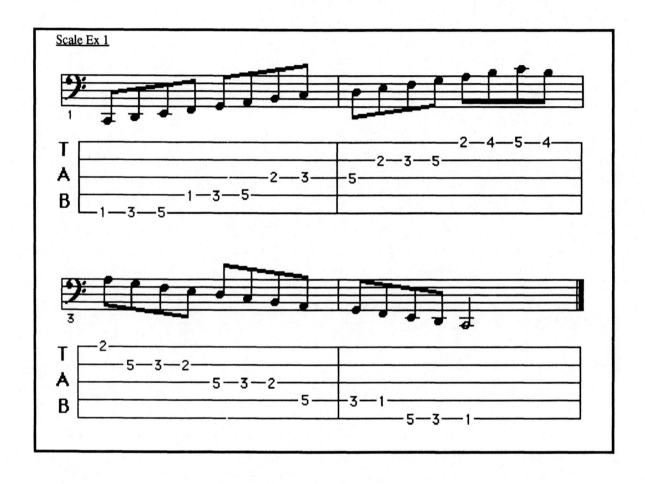

Scale Ex 2

MAJOR PENTATONIC SCALES..

The following **major pentatonic scale** patterns are derived from the major scale patterns learned in the previous section. Major pentatonic scales use the first, second, third, fifth, and sixth scale tones of the major scale. Since the fourth and seventh scale tones are omitted, we will learn the major pentatonic scale in five positions, plus the position that is one octave above the first position. This is a total of six positions, covering all possible major pentatonic scale positions for those scales rooted on the 5th string.

The **C major pentatonic scale** will be used to demonstrate these six scale positions. I also recommend learning the A major pentatonic scale based on the two A major scale patterns studied in the previous section. This would familiarize you with major pentatonic scale patterns for scales that are not rooted on the 5th string.

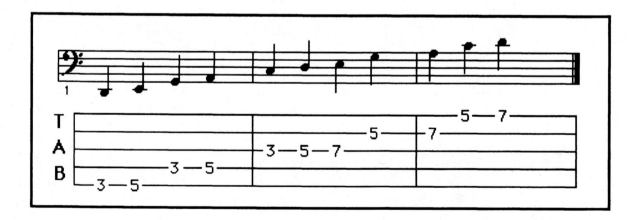

21

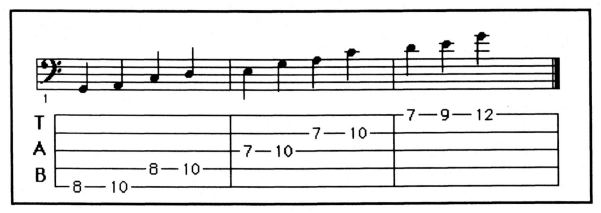

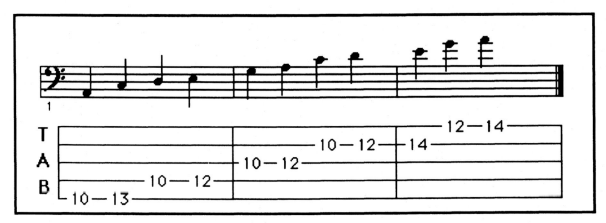

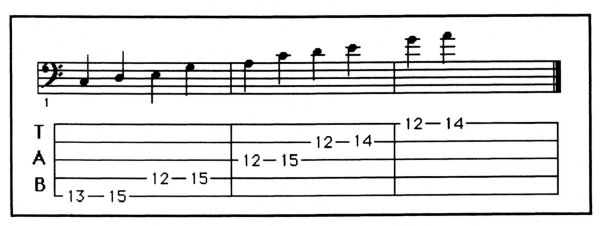

MINOR SCALES ....

The following **C minor scale** patterns show you how a minor scale rooted on the 5th string lies on the fretboard. These will be followed by the A minor scale to demonstrate the minor scale that is *not* rooted on the 5th string.

Also, don't forget to practice these scale patterns using the scale exercises shown on pages 19 and 20.

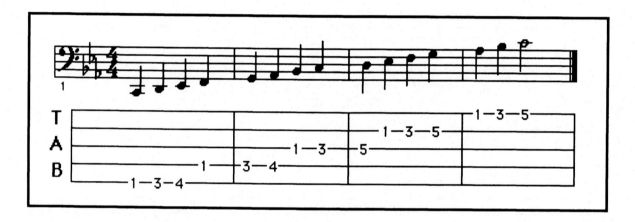

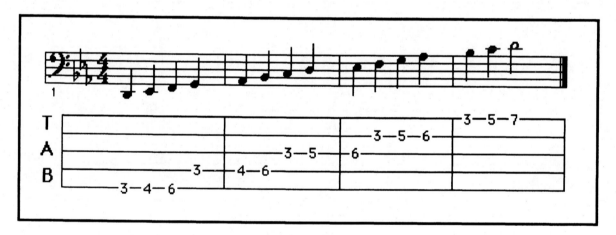

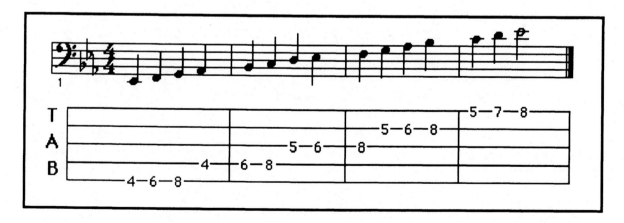

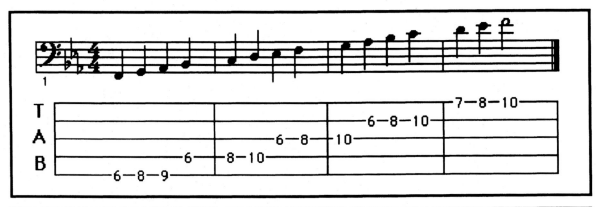

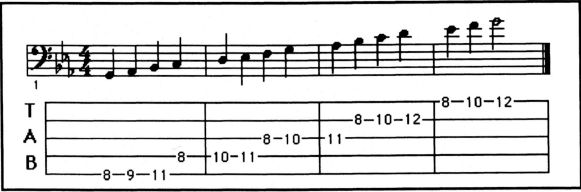

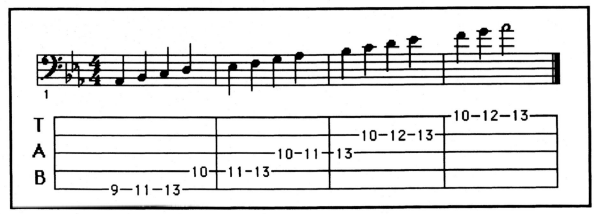

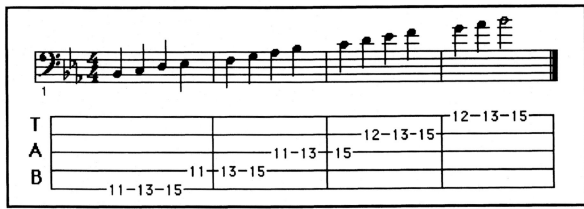

Here is an example of a minor scale that is not rooted on the 5th string. Learn the following **A minor scale** across all 5 strings in all positions on the fretboard. Also, be sure to practice those scale patterns using the scale exercises described earlier.

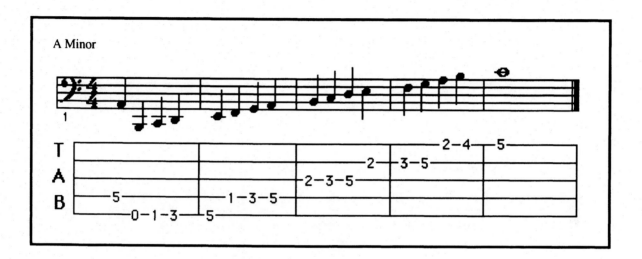

MINOR PENTATONIC SCALES..

The following **C minor pentatonic scale** patterns will show you the patterns for minor pentatonic scales rooted on the 5th string. The minor pentatonic scale is derived from the minor scale, using only the first, flat third, fourth, fifth, and flat seventh scale tones. On the 5-string bass, this five-note scale can be played in seven positions!

After learning the C minor pentatonic scale as shown, go back and learn all of the positions for the A minor pentatonic scale based on the 4th-string rooted A minor scale shown above.

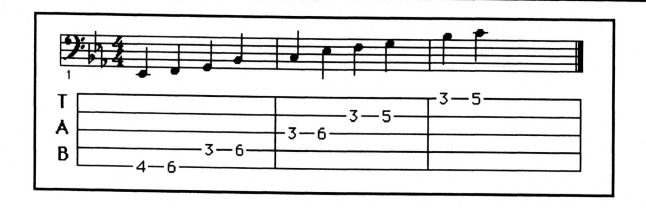

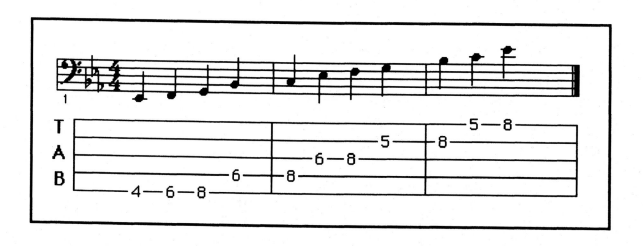

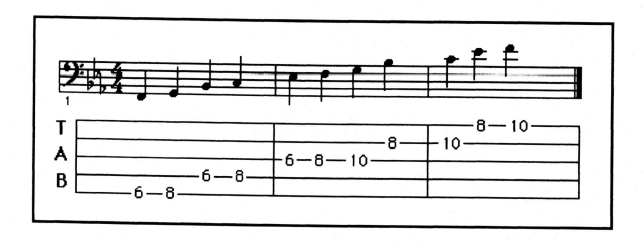

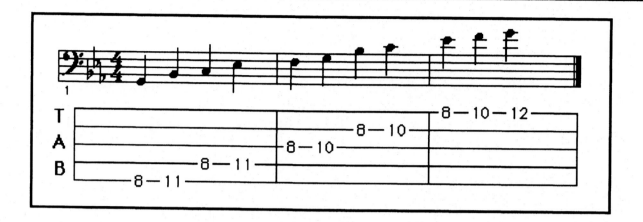

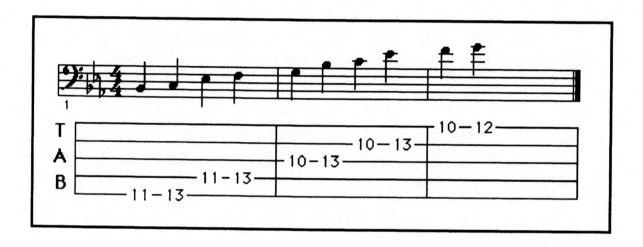

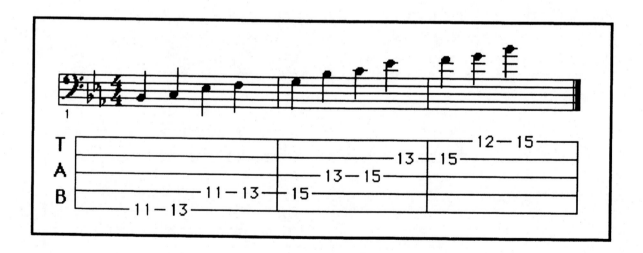

Chord Tones

Chord-tone studies are the next logical progression after learning scales. Since chord tones are derived from scales, the 5-string bass offers the same expanded range of chord tones as it does with scales.

For those of you unfamiliar with chord tones, they are the notes that make up a given chord. For example, the notes C, E, and G make up a C major chord. Therefore, the C major chord tones are C, E, and G. It's really that simple. The hard part is learning them in all positions covering the entire fretboard.

To do this, we'll take a look at five different sets of chord tones, all rooted on the 5th string, and one that is rooted on the 4th string. The five sets of chord tones we will learn are **major, major 7th, minor, minor 7th,** and **dominant 7th.** At the end of the first series of major chord tones, there will be an example of an exercise that you should use to help further your ability to run through chord tones. Be sure to apply the motif of this exercise to all of the chord tones we learn and all of the positions we learn them in (as well as any others you may normally practice).

MAJOR CHORD TONES ....

OK, our first look at chord tones on the 5-string bass will be the **C major chord tones.** The C major chord consists of the first, third, and fifth scale tones of the C major scale. This means that the C major chord tones are C, E, and G. To learn the C major chord tones in every position on the fretboard means to learn every C, E, and G in every position.

The easiest way to do this is to look at the C major scale *modes* we learned earlier in this book and pick out the chord tones in each position. We can do that. So, let's do it....

C Major (1–3–5)

C Major (3–5–1)

C Major (3–5–1)

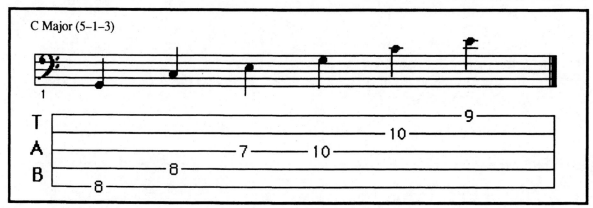

C Major (5–1–3)

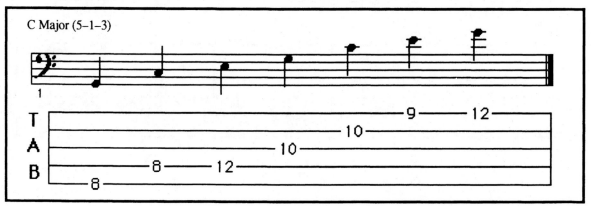

C Major (5–1–3)

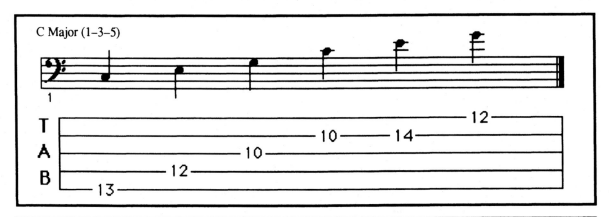

Now here is that exercise I promised you. It is shown for the Ionian mode (same as the first chord-tone exercise). Play each of the different chord-tone modes shown above using this exercise. This is a good one to keep you thinking while you play.

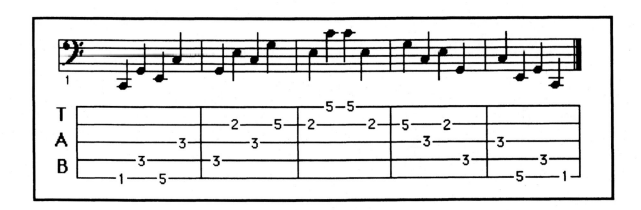

MAJOR SEVENTH CHORD TONES ....

Now we're cookin'! Let's not stop there....

Next we'll look at the C major seventh chord tones. These are taken from the C major scale, using only the first, third, fifth, and seventh scale tones. That translates into C, E, G, and B, which are the C major seventh chord tones. These will be played in the same positions as the C major chord tones, with the addition of the B notes found in each position.

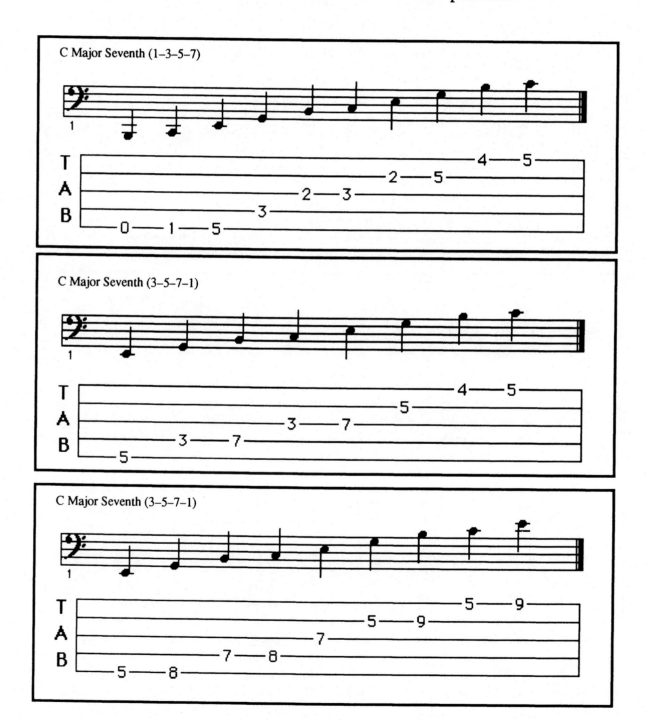

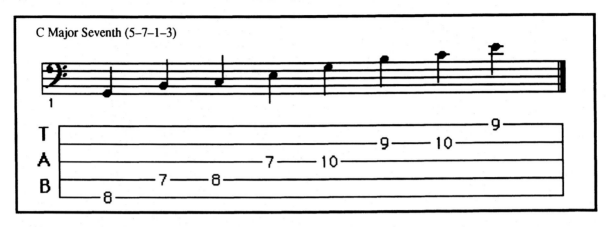

C Major Seventh (5–7–1–3)

C Major Seventh (5–7–1–3)

C Major Seventh (7–1–3–5)

C Major Seventh (7–1–3–5)

Here's how the previous chord-tone exercise would be played using the C major seventh chord tones we just learned:

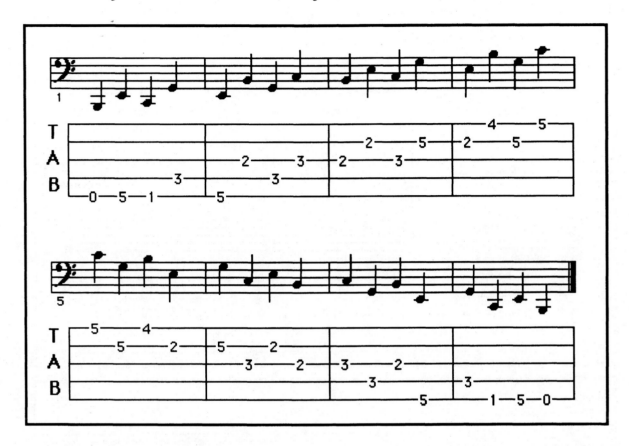

MINOR CHORD TONES ....

Here are the chord tones for C minor. The C minor chord tones are the first, flat third, and fifth scale tones taken from the C minor scale. That makes the C minor chord tones C, E♭, and G. As with the major chord tones, the minor chord tones can be played in all the same positions as the minor scale. So, without any further delays.....

C Minor (1–♭3–5)

C Minor (♭3–5–1)

C Minor (♭3–5–1)

C Minor (5–1–♭3)

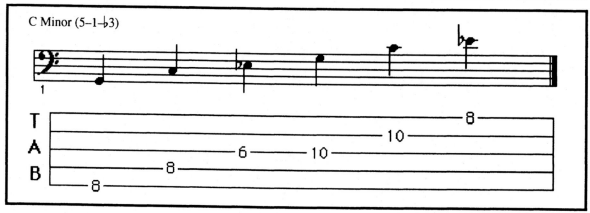

C Minor (5–1–♭3)

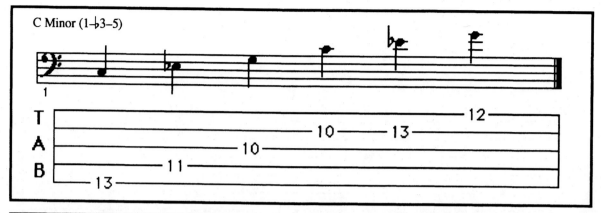

C Minor (1–♭3–5)

C Minor (1–♭3–5)

MINOR SEVENTH CHORD TONES

Minor seventh chord tones consist of the first, flat third, fifth, and flat seventh scale tones of the minor scale. For C minor seventh, the chord tones are C, E♭, G, and B♭. Once again, they are played in every position that the C minor scale is played in. Check it out....

C Minor Seventh (1–♭3–5–♭7)

C Minor Seventh (♭3–5–♭7–1)

C Minor Seventh (♭3–5–♭7–1)

C Minor Seventh (5–♭7–1–♭3)

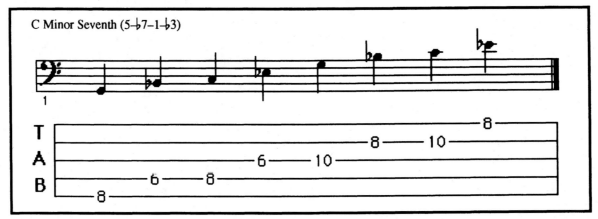

C Minor Seventh (5–♭7–1–♭3)

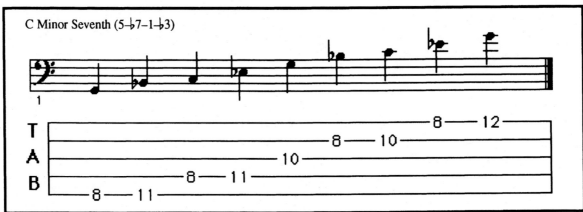

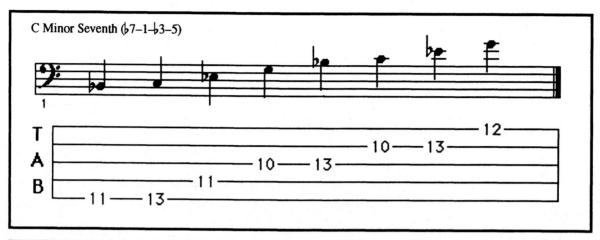

C Minor Seventh (♭7–1–♭3–5)

C Minor Seventh (♭7–1–♭3–5)

DOMINANT SEVENTH CHORD TONES...

Dominant seventh chords use the first, third, fifth, and flat seventh scale tones of the major scale. For the C dominant seventh (C7) chord tones that we are about to learn, that translates into C, E, G, and B♭. These chord tones will be played in the same positions as the C major scale.

C Seventh (1–3–5–♭7)

C Seventh (3–5–♭7–1)

C Seventh (3–5–♭7–1)

C Seventh (5–♭7–1–3)

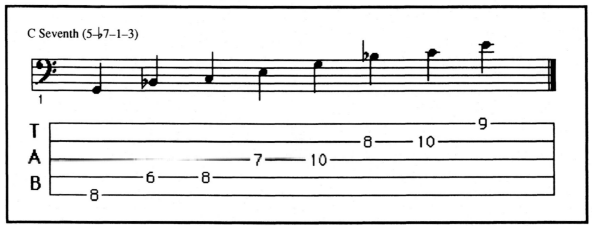

C Seventh (5–♭7–1–3)

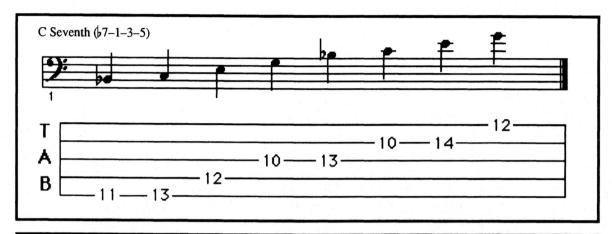

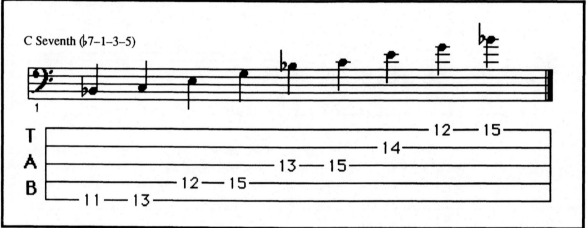

G MAJOR CHORD TONES

All of the previous chord tones have been *rooted* on the 5th string. That is, the root of the chord has been played on the 5th string (usually the first or second note of the first position).

The following **G major chord tones** will show you how to play the major chord tones for those chords that are *not rooted* on the 5th string. I have chosen G major to take advantage of the open B string, which will be used when playing in G major. Based on previous chord-tone and scale exercises in this book, you should be able to expand the G major chord tones to cover the entire fretboard.

The notes that make up a G major chord are the first, third, and fifth scale tones of the G major scale, or G, B, and D. So, let's do it....

G Major (3–5–1)

G Major (5–1–3)

G Major (1–3–5)

G Major (1–3–5)

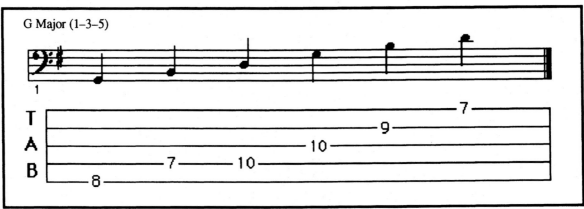

G Major (1–3–5)

G Major (3–5–1)

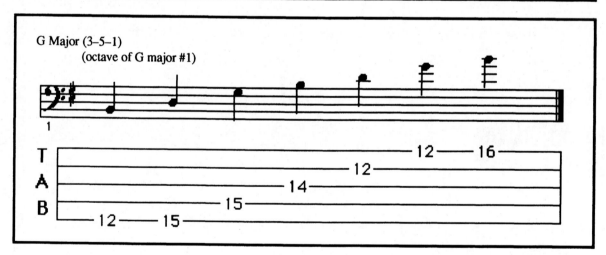

G Major (3–5–1)
(octave of G major #1)

Hopefully, these last two chapters on scales and chord tones have shed some light on the expanded range that the 5-string bass has to offer. This is useful for both soloing and for the everyday layin' down of that almighty groove! Be sure to use it to its full advantage!

Enough studying already! Let's have some fun! Let me show you a few tricks on the ol' 5-string......

Tricks

Now we're going to learn a few tricks that make special use of the low B string. We will concentrate on two different techniques that utilize the low pitch of the B string to fill out the "bottom end" of a bass line. We can do this by pedaling off of a note on the B string, or by playing a note on the B string at the same time as another higher note (also known as a "double-stop").

First, we'll look at some double-stop ideas, then move on to some octave-pedaling ideas.

DOUBLE-STOPS ....

As mentioned above, a double-stop occurs when two notes are played at the same time. Technically, when you play two octaves together, this is a double-stop. However, this is usually referred to as "playing octaves." Most often, a double-stop consists of two *different* notes played simultaneously.

Usually the lower note is the root, with the upper note being an interval such as a third, fourth, or seventh (although any interval will work, depending on the melodic effect you are trying to create). The examples I will present start with "octaves" and then change to show how you might create some melody using other intervals. This type of playing makes for some very "full" bass lines with plenty of bottom end and some nice melody moving on top of it.

So, here is the first example which uses octaves as the double-stops:

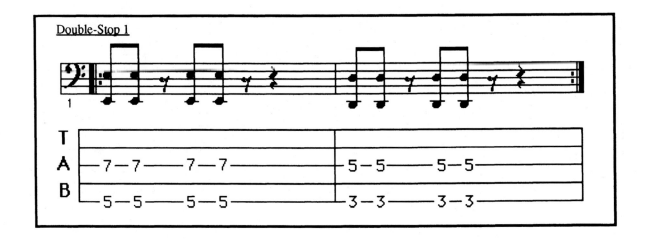

42

This second double-stop example uses both octaves and an interval of thirds, resulting in a line that creates a little movement by moving the upper octave to the third in the first measure (the E moves to G♯):

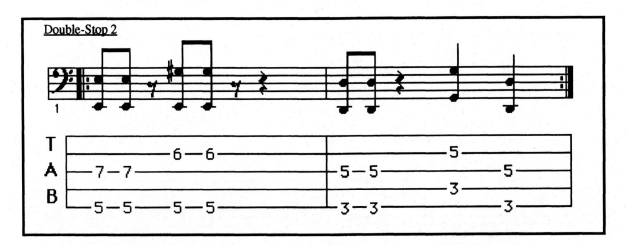

Finally, here is a line that again uses octaves and thirds to create even more movement. Bass lines like this can help "lift" a tune out of the same old everyday groove. Notice the melody created by the movement of the G♯ moving down to the F♯, then back up a half step to the G-natural. The use of octaves as the last two beats of the second measure works really well with a guitar playing a G chord to a D chord. All in all, this line contains a nice, simple melody finished off with the power of octaves, a combination that works well on the 5-string.

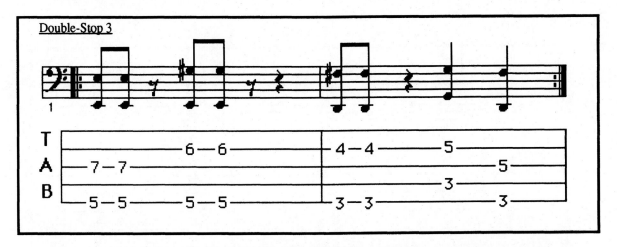

Well, that's a very simple and basic look at double-stops. There are as many double-stop possibilities as there are combinations of intervals. I urge you to explore and experiment with these ideas, as they will enhance your playing noticeably. Look to all of the scale and chord-tone studies we have already been through to help locate other intervals. *(That's why I showed 'em to ya!!!)*

OCTAVES ....

There are a few other ways to make use of the lower octaves provided by the 5th string. Many involve pedaling off of the lower octave, while others simply let the lower octave ring while other notes are played above it. These provide some subtle yet powerful characteristics to what would normally be a basic bass line.

So, without further ado, here are a few ideas for using octaves in a bass line:

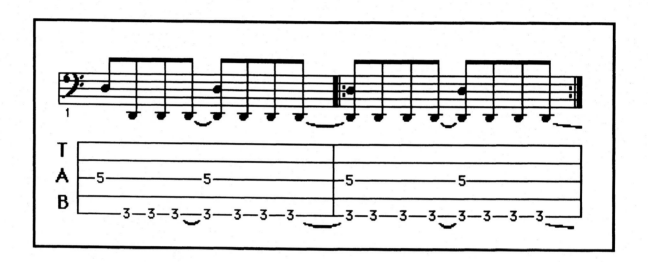

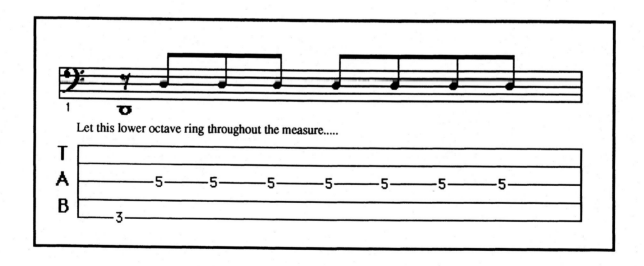

Let this lower octave ring throughout the measure.....

Let both octaves ring throughout the entire measure.....

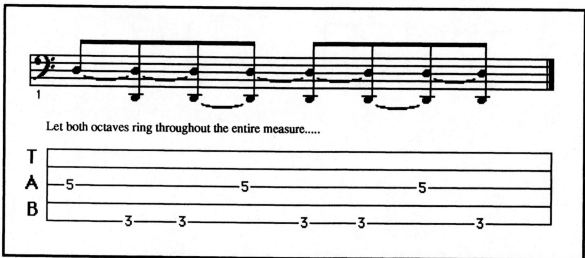

Let both octaves ring throughout the entire measure.....

Let both octaves ring throughout the entire measure.....

Let both octaves ring throughout the entire measure.....

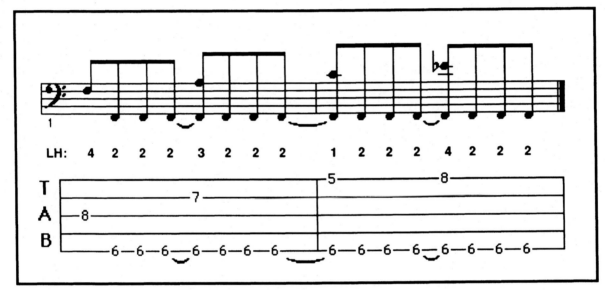

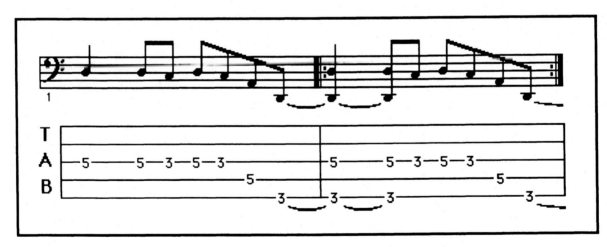

Slap Stuff

As with all other aspects of your playing, your slap-and-pop style will be greatly enhanced by the addition of the 5th string. One of the primary attractions of a 5-string bass is the ability to get a little further down into the lower keyboard range. In contemporary music, this means being able to play "keyboard bass lines" (usually synthesizer) on the electric bass. Synthesizers are neat, but ask any bass player and you'll be told, "There ain't nothing like the real thing!"

It seems that most synthesizer bass lines imitate a slap bass sound. Now you can reach those low Cs, Ds, and Ebs that synth players have been putting out. Here's some exercises and ideas to get you started:

EXERCISES ....

Once again, due to the "new" string spacing of the 5-string, we should run through a few exercises to get your right hand used to that spacing. Most players find that they need to be a little more accurate with their right thumb so as not to have multiple strings ringing as a result of each "slap." It is also a little more difficult to get the "popping" fingers between the strings because they are a little closer.

Here are three basic exercises to play. Don't hesitate to adapt any other exercises you may already use to the 5-string. Remember, anything that can be done on a 4-string can be done on a 5-string; and more!! Let's do it....

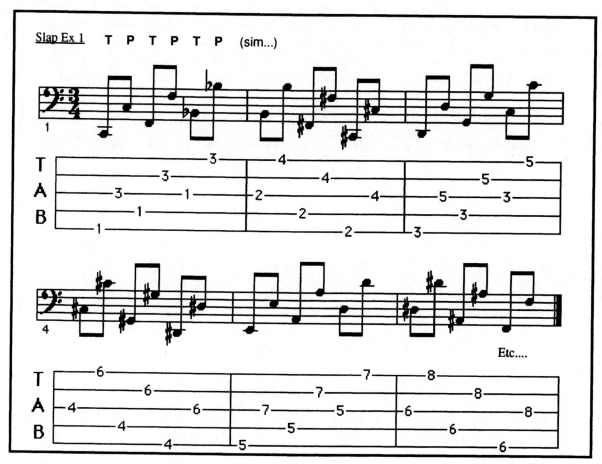

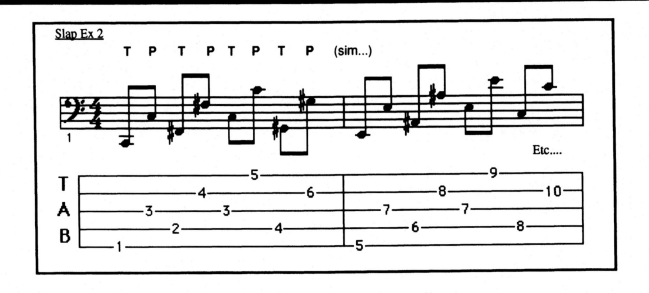

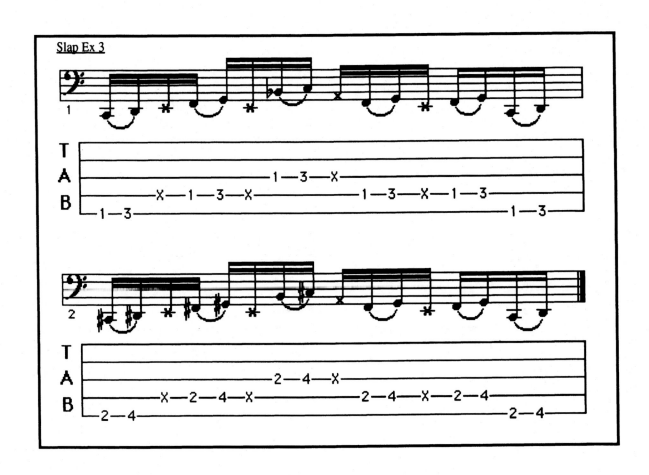

RIFFS ....

I think it's pretty clear what we'll be doing in this section. Here are some ideas for slap riffs using the 5th string to expand the "slappable" range. *(It may not be a word, but I can say it cuz it's my book!)*

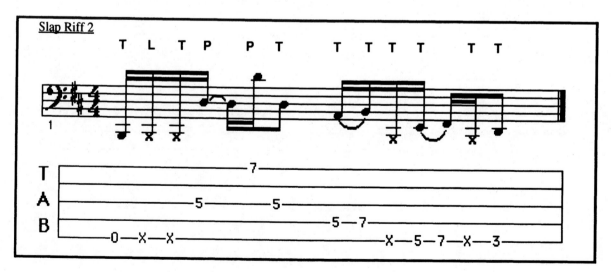

49

Slap Riff 3

Hammer-On/Pull-Off

Slap Riff 4

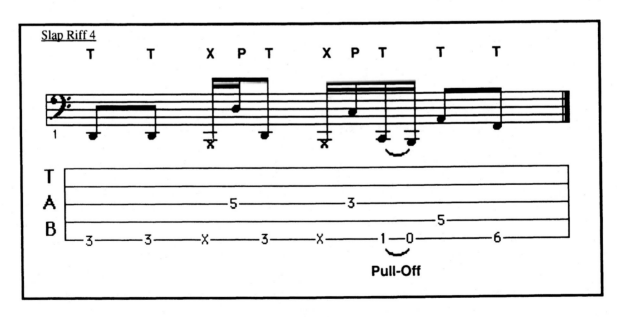

Pull-Off

50

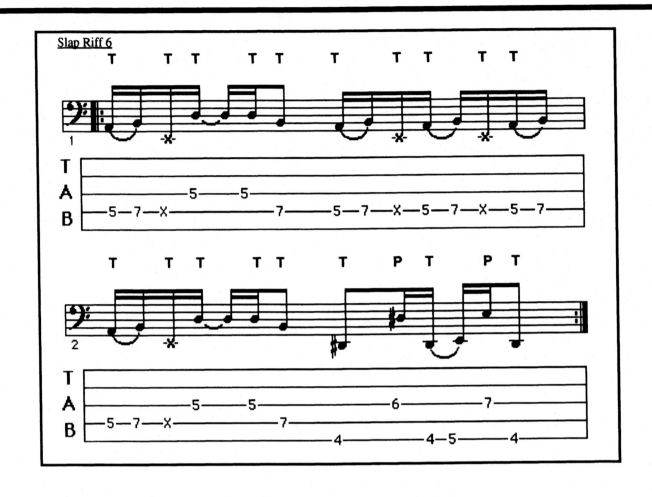

52

Bass Lines

To round out our "experience" together, I think it would be a good idea to present you with some different styles of bass lines as you might approach them on a 5-string. Some of them dip down into the 5th string while others are based around the 5th string. Hopefully, they will give you a good starting point to go off and develop your own 5-string style. Let's play some.....

COUNTRY BASS LINES ....

Here are a few country-style bass lines. You will notice the advantage the 5-string adds to root-fifth type of patterns in the keys of A, C, D, and G. The 5th string allows you to get down to those low notes that you normally have to go up to. And when it comes to walking country bass, why, you simply have more *walking room!* Check it out:

Country 2

Country Bass Line in G Major

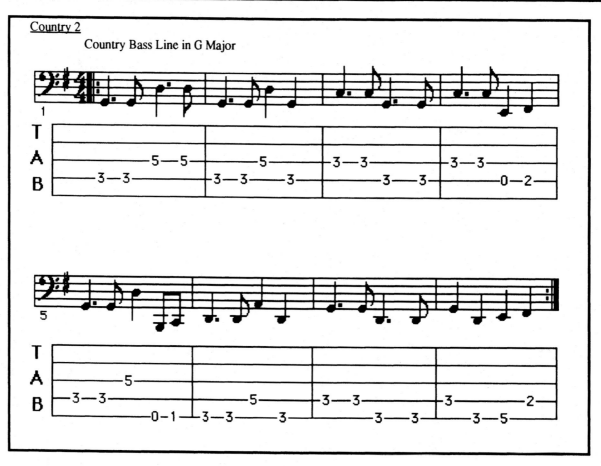

Country 3

Country Walking Bass Line in A Major

Country Walking Bass Line in G Major

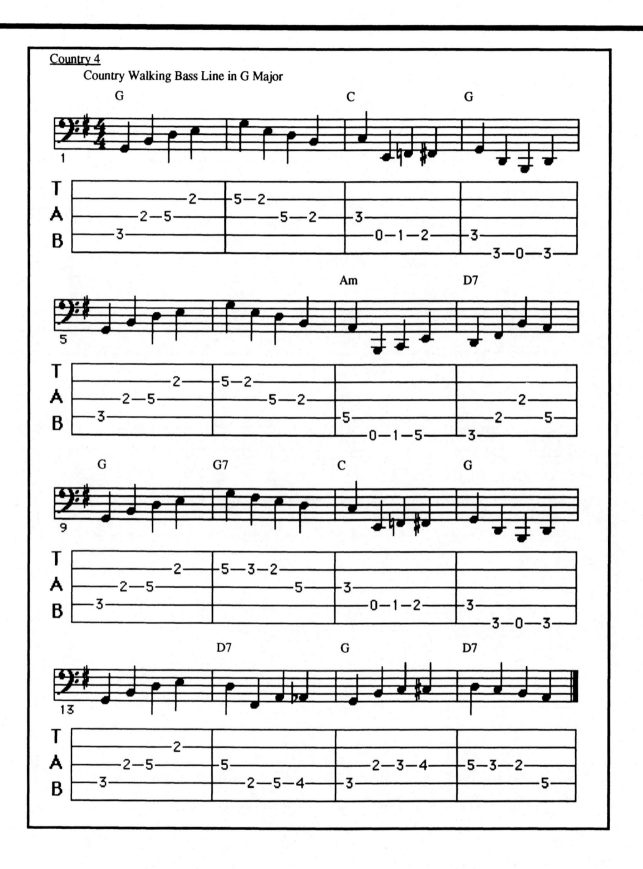

ROCK BASS LINES ....

Let's rock!! Rock bass lines can be tremendously enhanced by really grabbing those low notes down on the 5th string and making them *growl!* Let's try it....

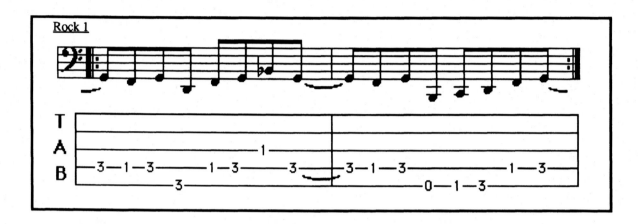

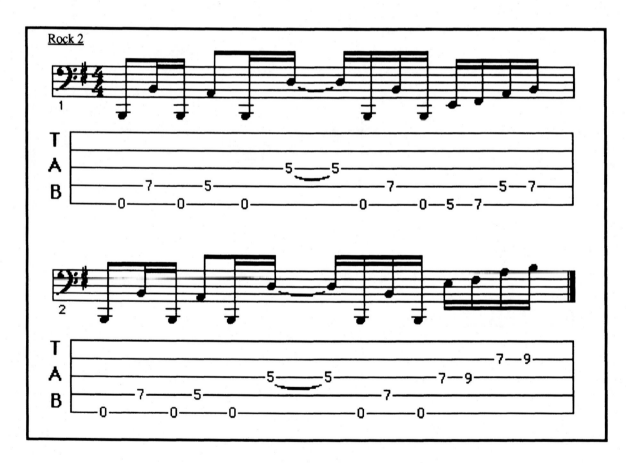

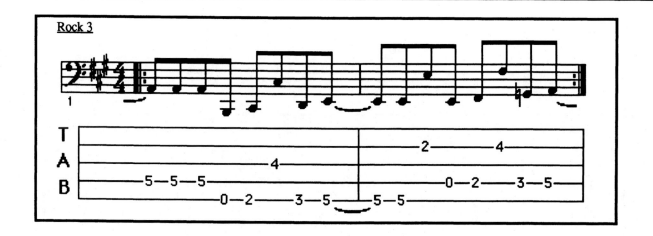

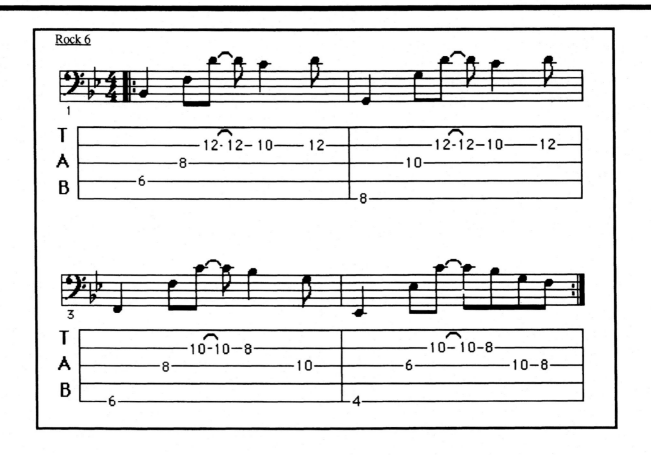

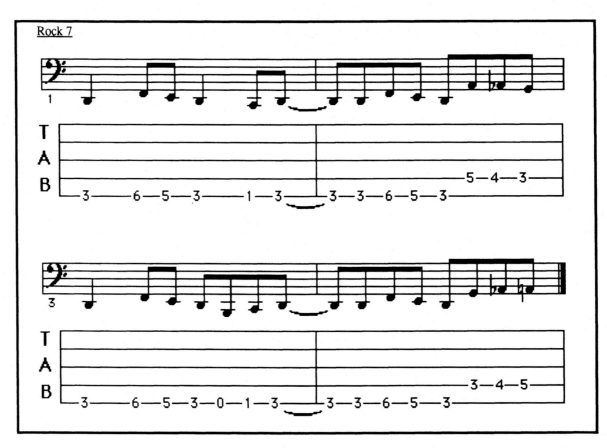

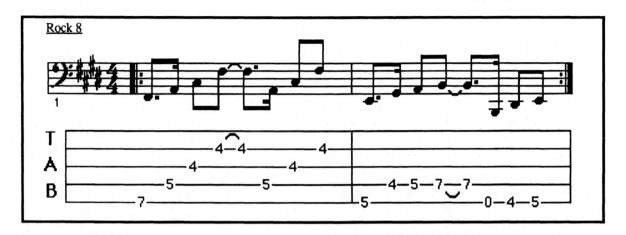

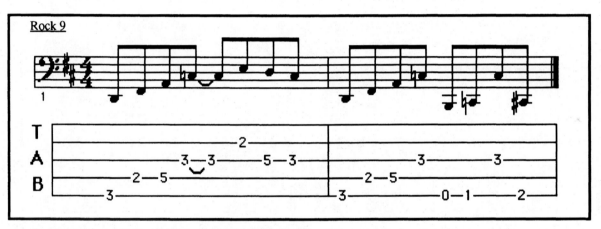

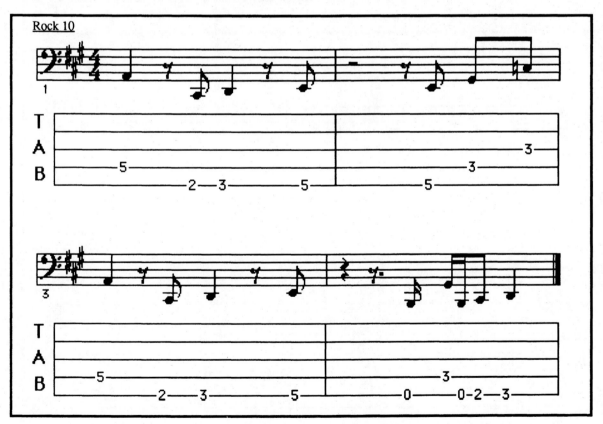

WALKING BASS LINES..

Finally, here are a few walking bass lines to get you walkin' all over that 5th string!

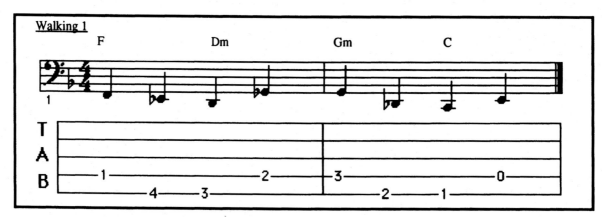

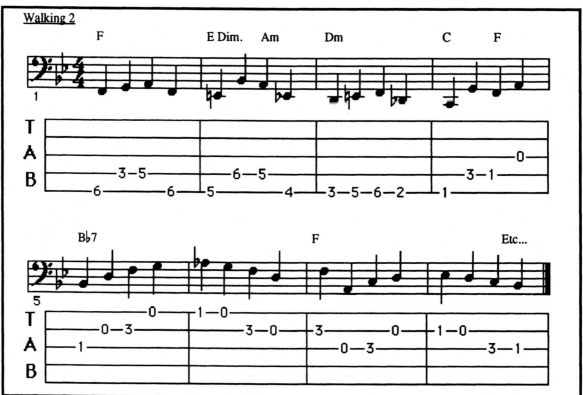

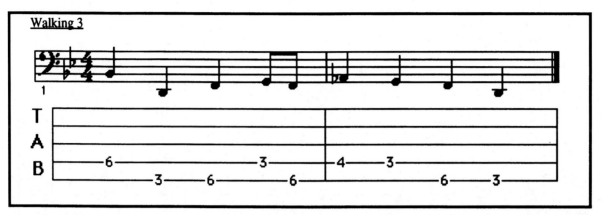

Walking 3

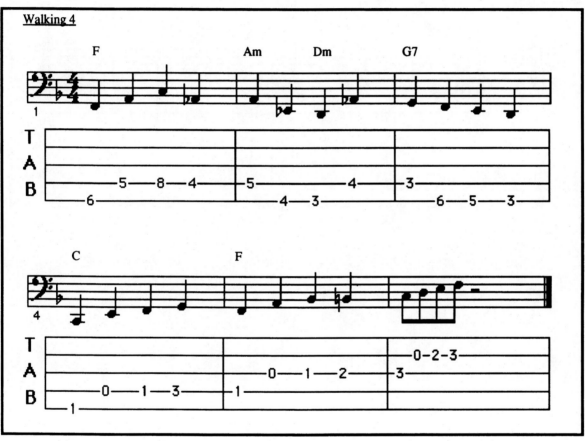

Walking 4

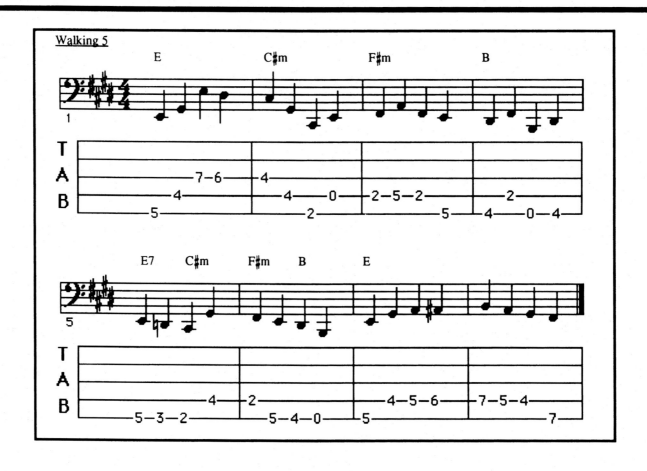

Last Word...

Well, I hate long good-byes, so I'll try to keep this short. I hope that I have been able to show you some things that will help your 5-string playing be as good and as exciting as you want it to be. I have tried to plant some seeds and give you some things with which to experiment. Remember, anything that can be done on a 4-string bass can be done on a 5-string bass — sometimes a little deeper!

The 5-string bass is here to stay. If you're serious about your playing, make sure that when that day comes that someone asks if you play 5-string, you can take the ideas in this book, combine them with your own creative input, and knock 'em dead. (*Then politely answer "yes."*)

Most importantly, though, keep learning and by all means *keep having fun!!* That's why we all do this, right? **Right!**

'Til next time........ B-Bye!!

.....Mike